Concoction

Immigration, Sex and Deceit

Nicol G

This book is a product of non-fiction. The characters, names, and some of the places and incidents are products of the writer's creation, experience and imagination or have been used fictitiously and are not to be construed as real. Any resemblance in name of persons, living or dead, incidents, actual events or organisations is entirely coincidental.

Preface

This book has a target audience of people above the age of sixteen. There are sexual scenes, which have been described in vivid detail. It is non-fiction based on the author's experiences and interviews roaming across Europe and Africa.

The story begins with the description of the main character Clement, and the challenges he and his family faced in his home country, Tayol. Life became very tough for them, as his father, who was the breadwinner, retired and became extremely sick. Clement had to then step up to become the breadwinner. When the family realised that the household income was insufficient, they decided, as a last resort, to send him abroad to Denmark for greener pastures.

Arriving in Denmark, he faced a new set of challenges living life as a migrant student. With luck on his side, he quickly settled in his new environment. He started dating Gladys, a lady he had admired a few years earlier while they were in Tayol. They quickly became lovers and she moved in with him. They had a bittersweet relationship. She became pregnant; but he wanted her to have an abortion as his career was more important to him than becoming a father. Would she agree?

TABLE OF CONTENT

Chapter 1: Clement, His Family and Friends

It is five in the morning; Clement had just been woken by his mother's voice, screaming at everyone to wake up. She went from room to room in the three-bedroom house to make sure that everyone was awake.

Clement's father, Richard hated this as the screaming woke him up too, but he was powerless to do anything about it.

For financial reasons, she couldn't afford to buy alarm clocks, which would actually have been the best way to get the rest of the family up in the morning. She did this every single day, unless she was sick, in which case she would assign this important duty to one of her daughters.

Clement, his elder brother, Eric and his three sisters; Clementine, Olivia and Mary, each had dedicated household chores to be carried out every morning. Some chores were to be done outside; Clement had to sweep the entire compound with a broomstick that he and his sisters had made using the leaves of a palm tree they owned.

Clementine's task was to do the dishes. There were cleaned in two massive basins, one to wash them, the other to rinse. There was no kitchen sink in the house or a dishwasher. Eric was responsible for collecting the water from their well, which was then used for laundry and for washing the dishes. Olivia and Mary were to sweep and mop the floor of the entire house.

Despite the fact that Richard earned a reasonable salary, he was quite conservative. Most of his money got used up in affording his children the best education. He sent them to private schools, as these schools performed better than the public/state ones in the nationwide examinations, both at secondary school and at high school levels.

Public schools were not generally well-organised or ran properly. There were frequent strikes by teachers due to low wages and unsafe working environments.

Therefore, Richard made the decision to send his children to private or mission schools. Consequently neither he nor the rest of the family went out much for fun activities. They often stayed indoors watching television, which became their favourite past-time.

Since Clement was still young, and since he and his family only watched the one available television channel owned by the state, he pictured Tayol as the best place to live on the earth. The state TV channel had made it a duty to only broadcast the positive aspects of the country. It was portrayed to be a country blessed with gold, diamonds, oil, bauxite, uranium, iron ore, cocoa, banana, timber, beautiful beaches and other valuable resources.

Most often, the programmes of how these natural resources were exported to other countries were shown on a daily basis. Watching this state-sponsored propaganda on TV didn't seem right to Clement or his sisters.

They often asked themselves why, despite living in a country blessed with these resources, their father and many of their uncles were struggling to make ends meet.

About 80 percent of their neighbours were struggling to make ends meet; only one of their neighbours owned a car, and 90 percent of the people in the locality did not even own a TV set.

Often, neighbours had to come to Clement's house to watch the television. Clement didn't question anyone on this subject, but he knew something wasn't right. Being a doctor, a teacher, a pastor, or an imam were considered to be the noble professions. He envied one of his father's friends who was a medical doctor.

He had a large BMW and lived in a very large, gated house. His children went to the country's most expensive boarding school and frequently travelled to Europe and America for vacations. He would often offer cash to Clement and his siblings when he visited them. For this reasons, Clement was determined to become a medical doctor in the future.

Finding Integration

He finally gathered the courage to ask his father why their lifestyle and that of his extended family members and neighbours was so low in standard as compared to the lifestyle of many others, as demonstrated on the TV. He asked if it was because of the city that they lived in.

If so, he wanted to know why his dad would not move to a different city where life could have been much better.

Faced with these almost confrontational questions, his father had to explain the reality to him. He began by telling him that most of what he saw on the TV was state-sponsored propaganda. He went further to explain that, yes life was better in the capital city but it was very expensive for most of the people to live there. He said they could not afford to live there.

He explained that the government had spent most of its resources to ensure that the capital city looked beautiful, with good roads, five-star hotels, well designed buildings and ensuring that is was spotlessly clean at all times because, that is where all the top government officials, politicians, the mega-rich business individuals and diplomats from other countries lived.

He said many international organisations, NGOs, foreign and African billionaires, foreign governments and private groups have been in constant attempts since the era of independence to promote regional development, food production, education, better housing, health care, improved infrastructure, jobs and economic growth in all parts of the country.

However, since the government officials who handle all these contracts were so corrupt and embezzled most of the funds, other parts of the country could not gain from such funding.

He said that this was one of the reasons why most of the news and programmes on television about the country were focused on activities of the capital.

His father then went on to tell him that while he was a student, he had studied about a research studies conducted on this topic and the various outcomes had different explanations for this misuse of funds; he said some of the scholars cited pervasive corruption of government officials and the justice system, predatory multinational corporations as the core reasons why the wealth of the country was not shared and enjoyed equally by all its citizens.

Clement didn't know so much about his country, and this was because as a part of his school history curriculum, instead of the schools studying about Tayol and its history, the schools were instructed by the ministry of national education to teach their students only about the history of European countries and the world. He said this was a tactic used by the government to keep the young Tayolese from being educated about their country so that, they would never grow to revolt against the government.

He then proceeded to give Clement a small lecture about the history of Tayol. He said Tayol was a country with a population of over ten million people and that It had fifteen states. He was informed that the official language was Matoh, although English was widely spoken and understood by most and that there were over one hundred tribal languages and ethnic groups.

His father then went on to tell him that Tayol has had only five presidents since its independence and that most of the presidents always wanted to rule for life, so they kept changing the constitution and rigging elections to stay in power. He was informed that the only ways the previous presidents had left power was due to sudden death or through military intervention and subsequent deposition.

Standing Tall for Family

Richard was a university lecturer, so he would often provide detailed explanations when asked a question, especially if the question was asked by any of his children. Nancy, his wife, was a housewife. She managed all the household activities and the cooking. They were very religious.

They wanted Clement and his siblings to be caring, loving, and obedient and not be judgemental of others. Eric being the first child, had been given all the attention in the world when he was the only child, which let to him developing a lazy attitude and a selfish nature. He was quite non-cooperative with his siblings.

Clement, on the other hand, was more hard working, he embraced every opportunity that was presented to him, and he was open to everyone and always offered help to his parents and siblings.

His younger sisters looked up to him as their role model. Growing up in his neighbourhood, he had a very close group of friends namely Patrick, Jude and Smith. Patrick was his closest friend. They had all attended the same nursery, primary and secondary school.

Clement's father earned a monthly salary of 250,000Kobas, approximately ($300). This was a decent enough wage in Tayol, most people lived on less than $1 per day. Clement's father's salary was decent enough to pay the rent, afford all household basics as well as his children's education in private institutions.

Being conservative meant Richard was very tight when it came to his expenditures. They hardly replaced any broken furniture or items in the house.

For example, if a mirror was broken, instead of replacing it, they would use a tape to patch it up. There was a mirror in Richard's room that had been patched up almost twenty times. He had used it from the time he was in secondary school.

It was about fifty years old. While this conservative lifestyle was normal for Clement and his three sisters, his elder brother Eric was not very happy about it.

He had grown up feeling frustrated with the fact that he no longer enjoyed the luxuries and attention he did when he was the sole child. It was as if he felt his parents should get rid of Clement and his sisters.

Patrick, being the sole child to his parents who were mega-rich and owned the only car in the neighbourhood, would quite often share his gifts with his very good friend Clement. They would play at the park, sometimes joined by Clement's younger sisters, but often, Eric would refuse to join them.

Eric always wanted his parents to offer them gifts like those offered to Patrick. Since Clement was of extraordinary good character, he was highly favoured by his uncle Smith, his father's younger brother and his aunt, Samantha; they all wanted him to fulfil his dream of becoming a doctor. They lived a mile away from Clement's home. He worked as a pharmacist and the wife worked as a self-employed trader. They had eight children.

Uncle Smith and his family lived a similar lifestyle to his brother Richard. Samantha had to work to supplement their income since they had many children, but she had to be a self-employed trader to give her the flexibility to attend to her children who were all younger than Clement. Clement frequently visited his uncle.

This was just to greet them as a matter of respect and to play football with his cousins at the nearby park.

Chapter 2: Clement's Future

After achieving exceptionally top grades in all his subjects at the secondary school, Clement gained an admission to one of the most prestigious boarding schools in the country.

He had to leave home for the first time, away from all family and friends from his state of Yobo to Boyambi, where his boarding school was located. The place was about 150 miles, but because of the extremely bad roads, full of potholes, too many police checks on the roads and many toll gates, it took them ten hours to reach.

He and the family were lucky for his father's friend drove him to the school in his BMW, free of charge. The entire family had the opportunity to accompany him to his new school as his father would not have been able to afford the transportation cost for the entire family if they had to use public transport.

His friend Patrick didn't do well at the state secondary school exams and so, he wasn't admitted in the same high school although his parents could afford it.

It was a very emotional moment for Clement as well as all his friends and family. He was excited to go and face the challenges and opportunities that were ahead but at the same time, he was frantic.

He had never been away from his family and friends and had heard quite frightening stories of how the first year of being in a boarding school would be grim. His mother felt like she was losing a son.

She was petrified that Clement would be traumatised by the experience, especially as he was going to a place where he didn't know anyone. The fact that Clement was obedient, hard-working and well behaved gave the entire family some reassurance that he would overcome all his challenges and go on to succeed.

The family was allowed to visit him once a month, on the last Saturday of every month. This was relieving to the family, especially for his mother and his sisters. His father had been to a boarding school, so he wasn't particularly worried.

He knew Clement would be fine once he got there and adapted to his new environment. Mobile phones were not a common phenomenon in his family. No member of his family had a mobile phone, so distant communication with his family and friends was done by postal writing.

Given the fact that postal services were not efficiently managed, there were exceptionally long delays in getting letters to him. There were no postal delivery companies and two third of household and institutions did not have any official registered addresses.

The school had paid for a postal box at the post office where all the sent mails to them were kept before being redistributed. The school would often send the official school bus driver to go to the post office and check if there were any mails and to collect and deliver them to the school administrators who would then deliver them to the students.

Due to the fact that the mails were not frequently received in their postal box, it was cost effective for the school to sometimes wait for about six weeks before they sent the driver to go and check for mails.

They were times when Clement's family would send a letter to him and it would take more than six weeks to reach to him. He still encouraged them to write as he loved to read the letters and kept them as souvenirs.

The Rigours of Boarding School

Soon, Clement realised that being in a boarding school was like being in a military training centre that he had watched on television. Every activity was programmed and team work was the key to leading a comfortable life. Discipline was the primary motto of the school.

Any indiscipline was met with heavy manual work as punishment. The official communication language on the campus was English. Clement and some of his friends were caught on a few occasions speaking the Matoh language, which was forbidden on the school campus and they were punished severely. He had to split a dozen bundles of hard Iroko wood with an axe.

This was a very bad experience for him as this gave him blisters on his hands for the first time in his life. The pain from the blisters lasted for two weeks. During this time, he had difficulties cleaning his dresses as his laundry was done by hand. They were no launderettes on the campus.

The wood that he split into small pieces was later used by the school chefs as fuel for cooking the food for over one thousand other students in the school. The punishment was very harsh but the administrators of the school had approved it.

The administrators highly approved of these methods of punishment because the money that would have been used to pay for professional wood splitters went into their private accounts. Most of the students who went against the rules and regulations of the school were punished in a similar manner.

Another severe punishment inflicted upon Clement during his entire time at the school of which the school administrators had approved of was for him to mop the entire floor of the school auditorium.

He was punished because he had been late for a drama lesson. He was also punished once to trim a quarter of a lawn, the size of a football field. Since there were no lawnmowers, he did this with a machete. Clement faced this punishment for being late to the morning devotion. Being late to morning devotions was considered a very serious offense.

From waking up at five in the morning to doing his morning chores, everything he did was a routine. For him, it was not an issue (unlike his classmates) as he had grown up doing such routine chores at home. By the end of the first month in the school, fifteen of his classmates could not cope and left for other schools.

Academic Brilliance and Other Skills

Clement did very well at high school and graduated with A-grades in five of his six subjects; Biology, Chemistry, Physics, Mathematics, Religion and Further Mathematics. He then had to write a national entrance examination so as to gain entrance to the only medical school in Tayol.

He prepared well for the exams, wrote and passed the written part of the examinations but unfortunately, he couldn't crack the interview. This was a huge setback for him.

Prior to writing the examination, Clement had heard of rumours from some of his friends and it was later confirmed by his father to be true that there were some conspiracy theories nationwide regarding gaining entrance to this prestigious national medical institution.

The rumours were that due to pervasive bribery, corruption and nepotism, only about twenty five percent of those who gain entrance to this institution deserved admission on full merit.

Another twenty five percent deserved to be there, on merit of their high school results, entrance exams results but not because of the interview process. They made it due to the fact that they had bribed the officials running these exams.

The remaining fifty percent on the list were believed to have been recruited not because of their excellent exams results or how well they performed at the interviews, which were prerequisite for admissions, but because they were well-connected to the most influential people in Tayol. Clement had hoped that he would gain an admission on full merit.

Richard had informed Clement that there hadn't been any research proving that any students who made it to this institution and graduated regardless of how they gained entrance came out with the knowledge and skills that weren't of the highest standard.

But again, he believed that he could not completely rule it out that all graduates had met the right standard required. He said he had heard of rumours of students being offered passing grades by their lecturers in exchange of sexual favours and money at both public and private institutions.

He even told Clement that some of his colleagues who were lecturers at the University where he taught had confessed while drunk of haven offered pass grades to students in exchange for sexual favours.

Richard went further to say that he believed the high rate of mortality in Tayol was due to misdiagnosis of diseases by unqualified health personnel working at some of the country's hospitals and the lack of proper training on the use of medical tools and equipments.

He would not rule out the fact that some of these misdiagnosis that actually resulted in deaths in the country were the direct result of the corrupt nature of the recruitment process of students into these institutions and the corrupt nature of the lecturers and leaders of these institutions who validated the student results knowing that the students didn't deserved pass grades.

Richard said all of these things partly because he didn't want the result to affect Clement's confidence.

He simply had to do everything he could to put the blame somewhere else. He went further to say that the majority of the pubic in Tayol, especially the ones from poor households, were those who suffered as a result. This, he said, was because when the top officials in government, ministers, private rich individuals and their family members fell sick, they didn't go to the hospitals in Tayol.

Instead, they flew to hospitals in the European countries especially to the UK, France and Belgium where they were diagnosed and had high standard treatment provided to them.

He said that although these influential individuals could afford their medical bills, it was the taxpayer who ended up paying most of their bills for these medical trips.

This showed how a majority of those who were disadvantaged because of lack of financial power or connection with top government official continued to stay disadvantaged while those at the top of government continued to be at an advantageous positions.

Even with these details provided to Clement by his father, he believed this was huge setback. He was devastated. He had never experienced failure in his life time and his dream of becoming a medical doctor was being eroded slowly but surely.

He had well informed of the corrupt nature of the country by his father but had been hoping that with his hard work and with God's blessings, he would count himself amongst those who made it to the medical school on merit.

This was because he was a confident individual who knew that he was very smart. He quickly decided not to waste any valuable time and joined his aunt Samantha to help in her business while awaiting the launch of the next entrance examination. The entrance exams were only launched once a year.

During his time working with his aunt, he gained a lot of life changing skills and experiences; he became more outspoken, was more fluent in his communication, became very competitive, and took ownership of majority of issues at home where he lived with his parents and siblings and in making major decisions.

He was no longer afraid to take risks. More importantly, however, he saved a sensible amount of money, which he was to use to pay for the entrance examination into the medical school and also as a bribe to the officials running the exams and the interview of the medical school.

The next year when the entrance exams were launched, he paid and was registered. He studied extremely hard, both for the written part and also paid an agency specialised on employment/interviews so that he could gain skills in terms of interview techniques.

More crucially, his father had made contact with an official at the ministry of health who had confided with him that he knew someone who was a member on the panel that organised these examinations.

He had requested an equivalent of $1000 to bribe the interview officials so that Clement could get admitted.

As the money was readily available from Clement's savings, it was provided to the official just a while before he wrote the exams. These were exciting moments for the entire family. Once more, Clement's dreams were back on track.

He wrote the exams, passed the written part and was informed by an official that wasn't directly associated with the interview but who had connections to the interview officials privately after the interview, that he would be selected and that he had made it.

Last Minute Conundrum

One thing left him pondering; he could not be sure at that moment if he passed the interview on merit or based on the bribe they had provided to the official at the ministry. The entire family rejoiced upon getting the fantastic news. A party was organised by Richard and Nancy and family and friends were invited.

These celebrations were, however, to be short-lived. This is because when the list of the one hundred candidates who had made it was published on one of the main newspapers in the country, Clement's name was not on the list.

All attempts to reach the initial official who had collected the bribe directly from Clement's father went in vain and because mobile phones were uncommon, it was more difficult to reach the official.

After two days of trying to reach the official, they were informed that he had been killed during a shootout with the police at a local hotel.

Clement and the family were informed that he had taken bribes from more than ten people and had been planning to use the money to travel to the United States of America.

Unfortunately for the official, he was denied a visa. Following a tip-off to the police by a hotel staff at the hotel where he was hiding, the police went there to arrest him but he fired his pistol at them, which he had bought illegally.

Following ten minutes of intense shootout of gun fire exchanges with the police, he was eventually shot dead. He was the only hurt in the shootout. The worst news that was to come out of this was that, following the official's dead, Clement and his family had no hopes of recovering the money for the bribe they had paid him.

The police, after two months of investigation, closed the case with the conclusion that no one else was involved in the corrupt practices and that no money was recovered at the hotel room where he was killed or from his official residence.

They made a statement that through investigation and talking to his bank; it was found that he had withdrawn all his money and closed his bank account in the days leading to his death.

There were rumours that, the police officials, who had responded to the hotel staff call, had been seen taking a huge bag from the hotel after the fraudster was killed.

Notably, that was never put in the police report. Members of the public, journalists and those connected to the case concluded that the police had hidden the cash and distributed it amongst them. Unfortunately, there was no concrete evidence to prove this.

This left Clement heartbroken. He became very depressed and didn't eat or go out from the house for a few days. His father managed to convince him to try something else; to either work full time with his aunt or go to university for further studies.

With all hopes gone at that stage for Clement to gain entrance to the prestigious institution, Clement decided to apply to one of the state run universities where his father was a lecturer. He applied to study Biomedical Science and Medical Laboratory Technology.

The application was straightforward. He didn't have to write any exams or attend any interviews. Here, the admissions were based on high school results. Due to the fact that his results were excellent, he had no problems getting admitted.

He was lagging a year behind most of his high school classmates including Patrick who had gone straight to the University after high school.

This didn't bother him. He had still maintained his friendship with Patrick, Jude and Smith. They all hung out together, went to parties and engaged in other fun activities on their spare time at the university.

Financial Burden on Clement's Family

While at the university, Clement took specific interest to a former high school classmate, Gladys. He was attracted to her, but because he was naive and inexperienced, he could not gather the confidence to approach her and get a date.

He would often go to the library to study just because he was very keen to be an environment that she was in. She was always at the library studying. By the time she finished her course and graduated, he never had the courage to seek a date with her. He graduated a year after Gladys had graduated. He did extraordinary well and graduated with a first class honours.

Upon the completion of his degree, he joined a local clinic as a volunteer to gain experience working as a Medical Laboratory Technician. While volunteering, he continued to work with his aunt as a trader where he earned a good salary.

He moved out of his family home and rented locally just close to the clinic where he worked. This was because he wanted his own independence and also because he could afford it.

After a few months of his graduation, his father retired. Most of the financial responsibilities of the family were passed unto him as his elder brother Eric wasn't working or earning but stayed home with his parents, including his three sisters who needed sponsorship for their private secondary school education. His father also became very sick with arthritis and heart disease.

This was quite devastating to the entire family. There was now an increase financial burden on Clement. Following months of financial struggling for the family and himself to make ends meet, he had another breakthrough.

Clement gained employment as a permanent staff at the clinic where he was volunteering. He was employed as a medical laboratory technician. As a result, he had to reduce commitments and the roles he had to the business he controlled with his aunt.

The pay alone from the clinic wasn't enough to pay off both his and his family's bills, so he had to continue working with the aunt. With his father's sickness aggravating and the need for more money for the purpose of treatment, and with his sisters needing maintenance support for their education, the wages he earned from the clinic and the business wasn't enough to look after the entire family.

These things forced him to move back into the family home so as to reduce the burden of the bills on him.

This was only a short-term solution to the family financial problems as it helped reduce the financial pressure for a while.

The money he earned wasn't still enough to take care of him and the entire family.

With so much pressure, something had to be done to turn things around. He had given up trying again to gain entrance to the national medical school and with his father's medical bills piling up, he had to do something.

Europe Calling

His father, mother, himself, Uncle Smith and wife had a family meeting and decided that they should sponsor him to go abroad to Europe.

They believed that in Europe, he would study at one of the many medical institutions and achieve his dream of becoming a Medical Doctor. At the same time, he would be able to send some money back home in Tayol that would be enough to take care of his entire family's bills and financial commitments.

They chose Europe as opposed to the USA and other continents due to the fact that there were many European countries where education was still free for all. Countries such as Denmark, Finland, Belgium and Sweden offered free education at all levels to both the home and international students.

Talking of sponsorship, his father and uncle Smith decided that they would sell all of the land they had inherited from their father, use a part of the money to sponsor Clement's trip to study in Europe, the other part of it would go towards taking care of Richard's immediate pending and future medical bills, the household bills and the rest of it towards Clement's sisters' education for the upcoming year.

They expected that upon reaching Europe, Clement would be able to study while working and because the pay value of the Euro as compared to Tayol's local currency was astronomical; they were almost certain that with Cement would be able to send money to them.

Clement was spoken to about these possibilities by a couple of his friends who had already travelled to study in Europe including Gladys whom he had maintained kept contact with.

Chapter 3: Travel to Europe

Clement had witnessed first-hand how their lives and those of their families had been transformed from poverty when they had struggled to make ends meet every month to riches and being able to help others in their various communities.

He had been informed that it was very easy to find a job and earn money while studying and also of the fact that health care was free and available to every legal resident. To him, this was a massive dream, if he would make it to Europe. It felt as if it was a dream much bigger than getting admitted into the prestigious medical school in Tayol.

Clement suddenly regained his enthusiasm after the failures of making it to the medical school. He was determined that with the financial backing of his family, he would do his very best to make it through in Europe.

He was committed to finding a suitable university, medical school, country in Europe where education for both home and international students was free - where it was easy to obtain a study visa - and most importantly, a country where he would be able to live and maintain himself with the budget at hand and without any financial constraints.

Clement made it a duty to use at least ten hours, sometimes up to fifteen hours per week of his spare time at an internet shop close to his house to apply to the various universities in Europe.

He had specific interest in the Scandinavian countries. This was quite a strenuous and demanding task but because he was very determined and truly motivated.

He found those extra hours carrying the task very exciting. What made the exercise even more strenuous was the fact that Tayol remained one of the least connected nations in the world in terms of internet access.

Only ten percent of the Tayolese used the Internet, and those that did, paid heavily for the privilege. The speeds were extremely slow, so Clement had to spend twenty percent of his income on paying to browse the internet.

Internet shops had to shell out over sixty percent of an average individual's monthly income in the country for an entry-level fixed-line broadband package.

When he asked the owner of the internet shop why it was so costly to go on the internet, he was informed that, the reasons for the persistently high prices were multiple, complex and inter-linked.

He was told that Tayol suffered from a limited international bandwidth, a monopoly in the fixed-line sector, severely limited competition in the mobile sector, a regulator struggling to come to grips with consumer protection demands, and due to its week civil society that couldn't challenge the state.

From his research, he narrowed down the list of countries he wanted to study in to six; these countries were Denmark, France, Sweden, Norway, Finland and Belgium.

He had preferred the United Kingdom because of its well-deserved reputation world-wide for providing high quality and well respected higher education, especially in the medical field of studies but due to exceptionally high fees for tuition, living expenses and the extreme difficulty of obtaining a visa, he decided to stick to the six other countries.

He applied to numerous universities in the six countries with preference to Sweden and Denmark, even though France had the highest number of African students studying abroad. The reason for this was because he was fluent in both spoken and written English.

He found out that although Denmark and Sweden had their own specific languages, most of the courses in their higher education institutions were available in English, and that an average of 80 percent of their entire populations could communicate very well in English.

Moreover, the students' accommodations in the country were amongst the cheapest.

Within one month of making his applications, he received emails of acknowledgement from a majority of the institutions.

These were exciting moments for him. He could not share this excitement with anyone but his parents, Uncle Smith and Aunt Samantha because there was general suspicion of jealousy and witchcraft by family members and friends against individuals who were travelling abroad.

There were stories of persons whom Clement personally knew who had been murdered just because they had obtained visas to travel abroad, outside of Africa for studies.

There was a case wherein, one his classmate named Elvis was murdered, after he won the American Lottery and was looking forward to greener pastures and a better life in the USA.

As soon as Elvis obtained his visa, he immediately informed all his friends and family members. The family organised a send off party at his official family residence and invited close friends, former classmates, neighbours and family members.

After partying for a whole night till early morning, Elvis went to bed and never woke up. It was only later, the next day in the afternoon that Elvis's mother found him unresponsive after repeatedly trying unsuccessfully to wake him up.

They were to go shopping at the mall for items he was to travel with. He had already paid his flight and was due to travel in a few days. After an autopsy was carried out by their hired coroner, their suspicion that Elvis had died of poison which had been spilled into his drink was confirmed.

This was an emotional moment for Clement. He had to be tight lipped about his plans of going abroad to study and to have a better life both to his sisters whom he was so close to and to other family members and friends as they would get excited and inform others.

With strong evidence that people had been murdered in the process of obtaining a visa to travel to Europe, purely on account of jealousy, Clement had to be extremely careful.

After four months of submitting his applications, he received unconditional offers of admission from three universities; two of the universities were from Sweden and one in Denmark.

To his amazement, none of the universities offered him a place for medical training as he would have wanted. His degree being from Tayol was not held in high esteem as those from other universities in Europe, plus the universities felt they had to offer more places to their Home and European students before they could consider students from the rest of the world.

Instead, he was offered a place to study a Master's degree in Biomedical Science which was his second choice in all of the three offers.

He didn't feel too disappointed as he felt once he would travel to any of the countries, study and obtain his Master's degree, it could become easy for him to apply and obtain admission into a medical training course.

Admission in the SDU

After consultation with his parents, he decided to accept an offer of admission at the University Of Southern Denmark (SDU). This decision was based on the fact that he had some of his former classmates and friends studying at the university.

Gladys was one of them. There was guaranteed accommodation for all international students studying at the university, and because accommodation and living expenses were affordable, the tuition was free for all international students and more importantly since there would be job opportunities, the choice was much easy to make.

He was informed that some international students find employment in bars and restaurants; others distribute newspapers, work in telemarketing or get jobs where specific foreign language skills were required. He was also told that some students get lucky enough and find employment in fields relevant to their studies.

Obtaining his visa was a straightforward process, he received his admission offer via email, printed it out, compiled the necessary documentations for sponsorship, deposited them at the Danish Embassy and after one month, he was contacted through the phone by the chief consular officer to bring his passport and was issued his visa.

Even though it was straightforward in obtaining the visa, he had some minor complication in compiling the sponsorship documentations. The Danish Embassy required an individual attending higher educational program and who was not to pay tuition fees, and had not been granted a Danish State Scholarship, had to provide proof he/she would support him/herself financially while in Denmark.

Bank statements from accounts in some Asian and African countries; Tayol being one of the African countries listed, were not accepted unless the bank had a European branch. These statements of some local and nationwide banks of these countries were not accepted since there was notoriety of corruption and bribery to bank officials who confirmed fake bank statements to Danish embassy staff for being original copies.

The bank statement Clement had to submit with his application had to be the most recent statement in an account under his name only.

The Standard Chartered bank was the bank identified as the bank to be used by Clement since it had branches in Europe. An estimate of approximately 16,000 dollars was required to be deposited in Clement's name as per the visa requirements.

To raise the full amount and deposit the money in his newly created bank account, some of the household electronic equipments had to be sold in addition to the lands sold and Clement's savings. With all the requirements met, it was very easy getting the visa.

Bidding Farewell to Family

After obtaining the visa, Clement remained tight-lipped even to his sisters, brother, other family members and friends. Only his father, mother, his uncle Smith and his aunt were informed.

He continued his activities normally as though nothing had happened, so as not to generate any suspicion. He decided he would travel to Denmark, one month before the start of his course so as to familiarise himself with the new environment and also to apply for jobs.

He had been informed that most often, many students scrambled for jobs at the start of the study year as the city was not as big as the major cities such as Copenhagen. It had just a few industries.

As he was told there were not a lot of jobs opportunities around the university, he wanted to go early when there were not many students around, so that his chances of landing a job would be high.

After buying his one-way flight ticket, it was time for him to inform his sisters and brother of his travel plans. Even then, he still lied to them. He didn't completely tell them that he had obtained a visa; he told them that he had applied for a visa and was waiting for a decision from the Embassy.

He asked them not to inform anyone. During the period leading to the date of his flight, he spent most of his time visiting friends and family members. He didn't tell them of his plans but for him, that was the simple way of indirectly saying goodbye to them. He waited until two days to the flight date, when he finally broke his silence and informed his sisters and brother.

His father and mother had told him that it was entirely up to him when to decide to inform them. He thought they would be so emotional in a sad way to see him go, but they weren't. They were so ecstatic, jumping uncontrollably while hugging him.

They planned that he would be accompanied at the airport by his parents, sisters, brother, Uncle Smith and his aunt.

When they decided not to have a send-off party so as not to draw any attention, Clementine proposed that they organise a house party and invite a few family members and friends and tell them that the party was to celebrate Clement passing his probationary period at work.

He had passed his probation a few months earlier but didn't organise any party to celebrate it due to lack of funds and because he was confident he would not be long at the Clinic as he was already planning to travel and study abroad.

Since his parents were religious, they did not want to lie. They came under pressure from their five united children to allow them to do the lying. For Clement, his brother and sisters, the fact that he was going abroad to study in Denmark was news more massive than being admitted into the prestigious Tayol medical training school.

Given the fact that the family had celebrated when they received the false news that Clement had made it into the prestigious medical school, they felt his going to Denmark also deserved a massive celebration. Even if it meant they had to lie about the actual purpose of the party as they did.

To ensure that the party was grandiose, his sisters and brother broke their piggy banks, withdrew all the money they had been saving for at least five years each and gave it to Clement.

They wanted him to add to what their parents had given him as contribution for the organisation of the occasion so that he could buy enough drinks and food for the occasion. The occasion took place brilliantly without any incident or suspicion from any friends or family members who didn't know about his plans of travelling to Denmark.

He received so many congratulatory messages on the day of the occasion, even from his manager at the Clinic where he was working, as he was present at the occasion.

The manager too was kept in the dark about the real reason for the party. His presence at the party actually helped in making sure no one suspected them, as he was able to confirm to everyone that Clement had passed his probation in a speech that he presented at the occasion.

A day after the occasion, on the morning of the flight, he called and informed the Clinic of his resignation. He spoke to his manager and thanked him for the support and overall pleasant experience he was rendered during his time at the Clinic.

Clement informed him the reason for his resignation was because he was travelling abroad for further studies and was hoping to return as a doctor and to work at the Clinic.

His manager was shocked, but understood why he would have been lied to about the occasion that he attended at Clement's house. He also called other friends and family members to inform them. These calls were made at the airport in the presence of his immediate family members who had accompanied him, just three hours to his departure.

Some of his extended family members were very shocked and reacted angrily over the phone that he had lied to them about the occasion, which they attended at his house.

To calm them down, he told them that he didn't lie and that he had indeed passed his probation and that it was true but that he didn't want to tell them about the journey to Denmark as it would have generated too much excitement within the extended family members which could have lead to many non family members knowing of his plans, which could in turn, have put his life in danger.

He even told them that, he had only informed his sisters two days before his flight. With those words, every family member he had spoken to who had been angry became calm and wished him a safe journey.

Just before he left his family to go and board his flight, there was one final advice given to him by Uncle Smith, in his words, "Do not marry a foreigner like others do". Clement and his brother laughed but he knew that Uncle Smith wasn't just joking, being a very conservative man like his father.

When the time for departure came, he hugged everyone, his mother prayed for him to have a safe journey and for God to protect him while he was in Denmark and then he left.

They were all shedding tears of joy, especially his mother, sisters and Aunt Samantha. His dad, Eric and his uncle tried to be tough, but they too, had tears of joy running down their cheeks.

Chapter 4: Arrival in Denmark, And the Start of Life in Europe

It was a daunting experience for Clement when he boarded the plane as it was the first time he was flying; but he kept his composure. When he got onboard the plane, he had not checked his boarding pass for his allocated seat.

He thought he could sit anywhere in the plane just as he did when he boarded the public bus with his family to the airport. He had no idea that seats were allocated; he saw seats and cabins numbered as he walked into the plane and thought their sole purpose was to make it easy for passengers to identify their seats when they left their seating positions for any reason while inside the plane.

As soon as he passed the main entrance into the plane, he noticed a few very comfortable empty seats at the front; he quickly sat confidently on one of them just close to the main entrance.

Since he was smartly dressed in suit and sat confidently, none of the air hostesses tried to verify if he was sitting on the correct seat because they were afraid of being accused of racial profiling. He didn't realize that he was sitting in the business class section of the plane.

After about one minute of settling down on the seat, he became uncomfortable. He had noticed that most people who got into the plane after him walked pass him and moved to the back.

He did not want anyone to figure out that it was his first time in a plane. This caused him to be very shy to ask any questions to a tall, slim, blonde and attractive air hostess who stood close to him and was ushering other passengers into the plane. He decided not to look at what was happening behind him.

If he did, he would have noticed a massive difference in the level of comfort between his seat and the seats where the others were seated, indicating that there were different sections in the plane. But, he did not.

One of the hostesses who stood further away from him noticed that he was agitated. She walked to him and asked if he needed any help. He hurriedly said "yes, yes" and demanded a bottle of Guinness.

He was told there was no Guinness and was given the option to have a bottle of water, a cup of tea or coffee, a can of beer or a small bottle of whisky or wine. He decided to have the can of beer. Stella Artois beer was brought to him; he had never had it before and he liked it as soon as he had a sip.

Thirty minutes into the flight when the plane was on cruise control, people were allowed to take their seat belts off; he took off his own belt as well. By then, he had already consumed two cans of beer. He was more confident and relaxed.

He called and asked the air hostess why plenty of seats around him were empty. She responded by saying that most people preferred flying economy as business class was expensive.

At that moment, he knew something was wrong, he quickly retrieved his ticket from his pocket and had a look. He was shocked to see his ticket. The Air Hostess asked him if everything was alright. He quickly said no, that he wasn't meant to be there. He showed her his ticket and she confirmed so too.

He immediately confessed to her, he said it was his first time flying and that he did not know that there were different sections on the plane.

She asked him not to worry and that she would speak to her supervisor and find out if he could maintain his seat. She could tell from his facial expression when he glanced at the ticket that he was shocked and embarrassed.

She did not want to cause more embarrassment by moving him from there to his allocated seat in the economy class. When she explained everything to her supervisor, she was instructed by the supervisor to treat Clement just as she would treat any other person in the business class.

When the information was passed to Clement, he was so relieved and cheekily asked her if she could offer him some whisky. She agreed and served him. He felt more relaxed for the rest of the flight until he arrived at the Copenhagen airport.

He was greeted at the airport by two of Patrick's cousins whom he had contacted before travelling.

They were Doris and Martha, who lived just ten minutes away from the airport and had agreed to pick him up. He had brought some Tayolese traditional food with him; Garri, Smoked fish, Palm oil, Grind okra, Powdered pounded yam, Eru and Egusi.

Some of the food he brought was for Martha and Doris. They had requested it for them as it had been a while that they had not eaten a complete Tayolese meal.

He was later told that they had not been eating these meals because they were expensive to buy and cook from the supermarkets and that it was expensive to eat at the only Tayolese restaurant that was in the city.

Once he arrived at their apartment, the first thing he did was calling his dad and mum to inform them that he had arrived safely.

As they didn't have mobile phones, his dad and mum had arranged that he would call two hours after his arrival in Denmark to a phone booth they had located close to the airport where he had flown from.

They noted his expected time of arrival and boarded a taxi back to the airport an hour before his arrival, so that they could wait for the phone call at the phone booth. They were very happy to learn that he had arrived safely when he called.

Martha, on the other hand, was extremely excited to have her package of Tayolese food and decided that would cook Garri and Okro with the smoked fish.

Clement wasn't particularly keen on the food they were about to cook, for he wanted to eat some western food. He requested an alternative spread for himself.

Since Doris and Martha worked at a McDonald's restaurant, they had lots of hamburgers they had brought with them from work; so he decided he was going to eat the hamburgers as he had never eaten one before.

That was going to be the last time he ate one, he didn't like it as he felt the meat had not been properly grilled. Back home in Tayol, he was used to having meat grilled to extreme temperatures before it was eaten.

Cultural Shock

Martha and Doris worked the night shifts so they decided to take him with them to work so he could see the city at night and to see what they did for a living.

He was being very inquisitive and excited given the fact that it was his first time in Europe; he did not want to stay home on his own while they were at work. It was summer when he arrived in Denmark; it was the month of August when sunset happens around nine in the evening.

Since it was his first day in Europe and he had never experience daylight beyond six in the evening (In Tayol; the sunset most often between five and six in the evening), he thought his watch had developed a fault, when he looked at his watch and the time was 20:00 while there was still daylight.

When he checked the time with Doris so he could change the time in his watch, both Doris and Martha laughed. They could tell he was perplexed because the sun was still up at that hour. They had the same experience when they first arrived in Copenhagen.

He was informed of the time and he realised his time was correct, he could not believe it. Doris later explained that during the summer time, in most of the European countries, the sun takes longer to set and that quite often, the sun rise happens at five in the morning and it sets at nine in the evening. He was in complete shock.

At that moment, he knew there were a lot of challenges he would face while in Denmark. He seized the opportunity to narrate the story of his first experience in the plane, how he had travelled business class because of his naivety.

This generated a lot of laughter amongst them. Crucially, their discussions help them get acquainted with each other. On their way to work, he asked them what their roles were at McDonald's. Martha told him that they worked as cleaners.

This came as shocking news to him. He had thought they might have been working as food attendants or waiting tables. He was marvelled by the fact that, they being very attractive, intelligent and with a degree were working as cleaners.

When he was told that they earned approximately an equivalent of about $25 an hour (125DKK), he was even more shocked, especially given the fact that they were students. He was shocked because the pay of $25 was what the majority of people in Tayol earned per month.

The thought of him being able to get a job while studying and to earn enough money to send to his family in Tayol now began to seem more realistic.

He started thinking how he would potentially earn as much as possible to repay the money his parents had taken from Uncle Smith as part of the sales of the land and to provide them with enough money to buy another land similar in size to what they sold and also to pay for his sisters fees, pay for his father's medical bills and pay for all the household bills at his home back in Tayol.

They got to work on time, Martha and Doris clocked in with their badges and started the work immediately. He was amazed when they told him that being late for work on a couple of occasions, even by a minute, could result in disciplinary action and possibly dismissal.

Clement reflected on the fact that in Tayol, coming in late to work was a norm; most of the people did their jobs unsupervised.

He concluded that most jobs carried out in most sectors of the economy in Tayol were very inefficient, ineffective and most often, their work wasn't completed as per time frame allocated as a result of these reasons.

His final conclusion was that, this was probably the reason why the growth in the economy and productivity was very low; coupled with rampant corruption and mismanagement.

When they came back home after work, because Martha and Doris only had one bedroom in their flat and one bed which they shared, they had an inflated mattress which they kept for guests.

Clement was given the option to sleep either on the mattress or on the couch. Since he had never seen or come across an inflated mattress before, he was scared that it might burst off, so he decided to sleep on the couch.

First Day at the University

The next day, he had to travel to Southern Denmark where his university was situated. It was a journey of two and a half hours by train and cost him 278 DKK ($50). Doris and Martha dropped him at the Copenhagen central train station and he boarded his train to the University.

He arrived there without any difficulties, got a taxi to the university campus and met the student union leader who took him to a nearby hostel.

He was not particularly happy with this; he had already spent an estimated 600 DKK ($100) on the day for transport, accommodation and feeding. That was an equivalent of more than half of his salary he earned at his job at Tayol.

Even though he had spent a lot, he was not very worried because he had done his homework about life as a student in Denmark. He knew the cost of living was very expensive, and he also knew that the public transport, eating out and staying in a hostel or hotel was very expensive.

He was very fortunate when he checked out of the hostel the next day and the student union leader brought in a university sponsored van to pick him up. He did not have to spend for transportation. He was taken to the accommodation office where he made a one off full payment for a full year's accommodation.

At the accommodation office, he was very glad to learn that students only paid for nine months and got three months free accommodation within a year. The months of June, July and August were rent-free for students who decided to stay around.

In addition, he was also offered a ten percent discount as he was paying the full year's rent. This made him elated as he had made lots of savings from this and was now extremely happy that his entire year had been sorted for accommodation.

He was then later transported in the university bus to the student hall of residence. He had to go with one of the accommodation officers.

Due to the fact that he had arrived early than most of the students, he had the privilege of choosing the best apartment with the best view. After having a look around, he chose one of the best apartments in terms of size, view, free internet access, distance to the university (just five minutes' walk), cleanliness and the state of furnishing.

Getting His Own Mobile Phone

After settling in his new home, it was time for him to visit the city centre. He didn't have a mobile phone and all of his contacts were jotted down in his diary. He wanted to call all his family members and also to inform Doris and Martha that he had arrived safely as they had asked him to inform them as soon as he found a place so they knew he was safe.

At the city centre, he bought his first mobile phone; a Sony Ericsson k800i; he could afford this because of the ten percent discount he had been offered at the accommodation office.

He got his new SIM card activated and was very excited. He returned to his apartment where he made endless calls, informing every one of his experiences and how he had settled at his new place easily. He finally contacted some of the former classmates who were studying at the same university.

They were happy that he had arrived safely and since they were very busy with work, they promised to visit him over the weekend.

He needed to meet them as soon as possible because he wanted them to help him find a job so that he could work full time and possibly do some overtime work and then get a huge pay for the one month before the school year was about to start.

To be completely settled in his new environment, Clement had to search and buy a second-hand bicycle that he would use for transport.

One thing that had become evident as days went by was that the Danish people were very polite and humble. Most of the people he met and spoke to were always willing to help him with directions and advise about the local area.

In Denmark, bicycling was the most common mode of transportation; there were bicycle paths almost everywhere in most of the towns. Bicycles could be purchased either as new or second-hand from local bicycle dealers or from auctions at the police stations during the sale of lost property.

He was advised by some locals that the cheapest option was to buy from the police as they were auctioned at very low prices and that a lot of persons did not attend the police auction sales. When he bought his bicycle, which he bought at a local police auction sales, he had to learn to ride.

Knowing that Danes were humble and would help him the best they could; he took his bicycle to the park close to his accommodation, approached a group of boys who were in their mid-twenties and asked if they could teach him to ride.

They were excited to do so and after two hours of practising with them, he was confident of riding on the public roads. The bicycle he bought would finally turn up to be his main mode of transport for shopping, nights out with friends, going to the campus and to work, for his entire period of residence in Denmark.

One very important skill that stood out with Clement was his ability to research on goods and ensure that he only bought what was necessary and at the lowest possible price.

There were no price comparison websites online so out of the low-cost supermarkets around: Fakta, Netto, Lidl, Bilka and Aldi, he went into each one of them with a list of food and household items he was most likely to buy and did a price comparison.

When he found out that Bilka was the cheapest, largest and the closest supermarket to his student accommodation, he decided he would only shop at a Bilka supermarket.

With full knowledge of campus: library, computer rooms, classrooms, canteens, international office, he was now fully prepared for start of classes and life in Denmark. It took him just three days to be fully settled.

The next item on his mind was to look for a job. Although he was not personally under any financial pressure, as he had paid his accommodation for the full year, had his transportation sorted and enough money for food, household and study needs, he could virtually hear the imaginary sound of the clock ticking on him due to the financial pressure that he had left back home.

It was now time for him to demonstrate that he was very responsible and to take charge of all the financial matters back home.

Home Away from Home

On his first Friday leading to the weekend, he finally met his friends; Divine, Thomas, Gladys and Alex who had convinced him to choose the SDU (University of Southern Denmark) as his preferred place of study and who were also students at the University.

They had planned to visit him at his residence and to take him to their residence. He was so excited when he met them that he entertained them with some cheap Carlsberg Elephant that he had bought and sardine pasta he had cooked.

They were astonished at how easily he had settled and how fully furnished and tidy his apartment was. They were even more amazed when he told them he had paid the full rent for the academic year.

They found it very difficult to integrate and settle despite being in Denmark for over two years partly because they had travelled to Denmark without enough money to sustain themselves.

They said they were all living together outside the campus in a privately-owned accommodation in a single bedroom and that the landlord had let them stay together because he understood their financial difficulties.

More shockingly, he was informed that they were not the ones paying the rents. They had been under so much financial constraint and being unable to find a job to afford their basic needs when they arrived in Denmark.

So, they were left homeless and were forced to sleep rough under bridges and at bus and train stations after a few months of arriving.

They said showering was in café toilets and the local hospital bathrooms as there was no availability of free public bathrooms. Despite this, they had still managed to attend classes and stayed on campus till 2am in the computer rooms studying, chatting using yahoo messenger (there were no Facebook, WhatsApp, and Twitter) with family and friends but also because they had nowhere else to go.

Their breakthrough happened when Gladys, met a lady at the station who said she knew of a man from Tayol who had been living in Denmark for over twenty years and who could definitely help them. She gave Gladys his number and name. The man was known locally by his nickname Turbo.

When they called Turbo and explained the story of their misery since the beginning of their time in Denmark, he opted to offer them accommodation and to get them jobs so they could look after themselves.

He was a taxi driver by trade and owned five apartments. He offered them a room in one of his apartments, rent free and because he was well-connected locally, he had one of his friends to offer them a part time newspaper delivery job.

Unfortunately for them, there was only one vacancy. Another problem was that, none of them could ride a bicycles, which were not very common in Tayol and so, a lot of people did not know how to ride them.

On realising this, Turbo quickly bought them four bicycles with his money, took a day off work and taught them on how to ride the bicycles. It was very tough for Gladys to learn to ride but Divine, Thomas and Alex took just under three hours to learn. The job was officially given to Alex who was the eldest in the group.

It was an early morning delivery job starting from 3am to 6am and required the delivery to be done using the specially-adapted delivery bicycles that were provided by the company.

Even though the job was officially assigned to Alex, it was being done by all three men; Alex, Divine and Thomas who took turns of two days each per week from Monday till Saturday to do the shifts, since no newspaper delivery were done on Sundays.

As they explained to Clement about their life story since their arrival in Denmark, they took the opportunity to give him information about the newspaper delivery job and pay.

They informed him that as a newspaper delivery person, monthly salaries could be anything between 400DKK and 20.000DKK.($65 and $3200) The amount depended on how many routes the person adopted, how many papers they were distributing and how many days a week or hours they worked.

Alex told him that they earned 10000 DKK, approximately $1600 per month from the job and that the money was evenly distributed with Gladys.

Clement was informed that Turbo had offered the room where they were staying for free until when they had completed their studies and found their career jobs. It had been three hours since they started sharing their experiences with Clement; he had been left shell-shocked by their experiences.

When he asked them why they had not informed their families back home in Tayol to do something about their financial situation, their responses shocked him even more. All of them confirmed that a third of their earnings were being sent back home to help family members.

The thought of his own pressures to send money back home to love ones and family kicked in. He had heard a lot of sad stories in one night and quickly asked them to change the topic and talk about something positive. The drinks he bought for entertainment by then were nearly finished.

Alex proposed that they go to the city centre to one of the student bars where booze was cheap.

This was intended to have Clement experience his first night out to compare to the student night out in Tayol. They went to the

"Nedenunder" Friday bar which was a very popular bar with the students. It had a 600 square meter modern-looking lounge area.

There, they had a few more pints of beer and danced until the close of the bar at 2am. This was surprising to Clement because in Tayol most bars and clubs closed even late at 4am.

Sometimes, if there were still customers who wanted to enjoy themselves, bars would not close till 6am.So he was very disappointed to learn that the bars and night clubs closed at 2am in this city.

They went to the city centre by means of riding their bicycles except Gladys who could not ride. She was transported on the back of Divine's bicycle. On the way back home, Clement volunteered to carry Gladys on his bike.

He had a more strong and durable bike. Alex asked if Clement could stop by and see where they resided before going to his flat in the morning. He gladly agreed.

Falling for Gladys

He had been very attracted to Gladys when in Tayol and even more so when she and the others came to his apartment, so as they were riding home, with Gladys being on the back of his bike, he took the opportunity to have a private chat with her.

He asked her if she was the girlfriend to any of the other guys, to which she quickly said no and informed him she was more like a sister to them and that they now lived like a family.

When they all got to their apartment, Clement witnessed for himself their overcrowded single-room flat. There were a lot of positives from it though.

It was extremely tidy and neat and although they were overcrowded in the room, they had made it look spacious.

They had a double bunk bed with a desk, two inflatable mattresses, a Songmics L-Shaped office computer desk large corner PC table with sliding keyboard and 2 shelves of approximate size 70x60x40cm for studies and a large 2 door Bella wardrobe where they kept all their clothing.

Clement was informed by Divine that the cleanliness and tidiness of the room was as a result of Gladys' hard work and that they had come to appreciate her so much as a result.

She looked after them like a sister and mother on her own accord and was continuing to do so. His final impression was that their standard of living wasn't too bad when compared to what they told him when they met him because he had now seen the flat for himself and from their interaction with each other; he had seen that they had managed to live in harmony and appreciated each other.

The division of labour had worked well for them. While the boys worked hard to provide the income to fund their expenses, Gladys made sure that the flat was well looked after and cooked the meals.

As a result of this coordination, they could study without any stress and were still in a position of strength to send money back home to their respective families.

After spending the rest of the night with them drinking in their flat, he left early next morning and rode home to his place.

On his way home, he could not stop thinking about Gladys. He came to terms with the fact that he had been instantaneously attracted to her. She was five feet tall, very fair in complexion, had a big round butt shaped like an apple and was genuinely down to earth. In addition she was very intelligent.

She was also very polite and very respectful to everyone she came in contact with. Whenever she spoke, her words were replete with pearls of wisdom.

Quite remarkably, no one ever interrupted her when she talked given that she always spoke sensibly with precision. He just felt she was a ten pointer. Due to the hangover, he went straight to bed when he arrived home.

Later that evening, he decided to visit them. One reason was to talk about how they could help him get a job; the other and more compelling reason was the fact that he wanted to spend more time with Gladys.

They were very glad to have him back upon his arrival at the flat. He asked them about how he could get a job from his own research online before he left Tayol; he inferred that it would be difficult to get a job without being well connected, especially being an international student and being unable to speak Danish.

Notably, they had been the ones who had advised him to choose SDU as his preferred place of study. They were also the ones who advised that he would be able to have a job easily as soon as he arrived here.

He politely asked them about their plans for him. Joining them as the fifth person in the sharing of their income from the job would inevitably have a great impact in each of their lives.

He did not want to be the one to disrupt their already establish routine and harmony. Equally, he was compelled to think about the financial pressures that would build up to himself and his family back home if he did not have any means of earning money.

Receiving the Breakthrough News

At that very moment, Alex broke the fantastic news to him. They were vacancies for newspaper delivery at the local firm where they worked and interested applicants had been asked to come over at the firm on the Monday for possible induction, training and start the work as soon as possible.

If they were offered the jobs, Alex would be able to retain his main job while Clement, Devine and Thomas would get jobs of their own.

They all made a promise that, if offered the job, they would share part of their incomes with Gladys. Clement did not have to contribute or share his income with her but he opted to do so because he felt all of them, including Gladys, were the reason why he was able to study at SDU.

Secondly, he wanted to be part of their already establish friendship. Alex knew that their probability of getting the jobs was high because Turbo had recommended them and also because the firm felt Alex, who was the main registered employee with the firm, had been doing a fantastic job.

He had simultaneously recommended his friends as well, being the only person out of the four of them that was known to the company officials.

They were eventually offered the job. Clement was so ecstatic that he immediately rang back home to his family and informed his entire family, but not friends and extended family.

Understandably, his father, mother, sisters, brother, Uncle Samantha and his wife Samantha were very happy with the news. He did not inform his friends and extended family members on the advice given by Alex and the others.

They informed him that, if he spread the news to so many others back home in Tayol, he would be making more enemies than friends.

He was told that, friends and extended family members would seek help from him as soon as they knew he had a job.

Alex then pointed out that he was not on good terms with most of his other friends in Tayol because they had asked him to help them with a little bit of money, but he couldn't because the amount he earned wasn't enough to make ends meet and to help his family. It was norm not to tell the real situation of life in Europe to the people in Tayol.

Alex did inform some of his friends in Tayol that he had got a job and was living well, sending them flashy and well dressed pictures of him while standing by very expensive cars pretending to be his, but he did not apprise them of the stark reality of his life in Denmark.

He did not tell them that he lived with three others in a single room and shared his job and income with them.

In order to avoid a similar scenario, Clement had to be tight lipped about his new job to those who were not his close family members. It was very exciting times for Clement and his new friends.

They were to do just three hours of work per day between three and six in the morning, which meant that they would have time to prepare and attend early morning lectures and to go about their school activities without being financially worried.

Furthermore, they would afford to send plenty of money back home to their respective families.

It also came as a huge relief for them because they were to work within legal hours and earned enough every month. International non-European students were not allowed to work for more than twenty hours per week.

A Nepalese student and a student from Tayol had been deported by the Danish Border Control just a year before he arrived since they had violated the conditions of their visas by working more than twenty hours per week. Being cognisant of that fact, he was very happy with his job offer of eighteen hours per week.

Studies eventually began just after one month of him being in Denmark. He had worked for three weeks and was looking forward to his first pay.

Since the first week in the university was mostly slotted for enrolment, obtaining the timetable, getting to know around the campus and classrooms, he spent an entire day on campus enrolling and getting his timetable because he had already done a tour of the campus by himself as he had arrived a month before the university had commenced.

His priority for that week was to make lots of friends, getting to know his lecturers personally, attend a lot of the fresher's party and more importantly, to try and get a date with Gladys.

Mission Dating Gladys

He didn't want to tell Alex and the others that he was interested in Gladys, as he didn't know if they would react positively or negatively to it. Since, he had never gone on a date; he decided to get some tips from the internet.

Some of these tips implied that he had to try and do what she loved to do, make her feel special so she would know that he really appreciated her, not to text her for the sake of texting, take time to get closer to her and show interest in her interests.

Armed with those tips, it was time for him to put them into practice. The first thing he decided to do was to try and get a one on one time with her.

However, it was becoming increasingly difficult to do so because she was always amongst the company of Alex and the others. Besides the fact that they lived together, they all studied the same course, went to the library together, did grocery shopping together and had formed a clique that was very difficult for any other person to penetrate.

He counted himself lucky to have been allowed into their clique. They had never allowed anyone to visit them before as they carried out all their activities together. Everyone who knew them thought they all belonged to the same family.

He decided to text her and asked if she could help him with his grocery shopping, so that he would know which ingredients to buy for in order to cook certain meals. In addition, he requested her to teach him on how to cook a certain Tayolese traditional meal which he said he was unable to cook.

She replied in the affirmative, stating that she would help him to do so. Knowing that this was the best opportunity he had to gain her love and to be able to express his interest in her, he decided that he would not waste any more time as he might not have an opportunity to call her and to book a date and time.

They agreed to meet on campus as she had an appointment with one of her lecturers to discuss her thesis and from there walk to Bilka shop, the low-price supermarket which was about twenty-five minutes walk from Clement's apartment.

While he was overjoyed, he was not nervous. He did not sleep enough on the night before the Wednesday of the Rendezvous, as he was constantly thinking about the meeting he would have the next day with Gladys.

On the Wednesday of the rendezvous, he woke up very early, cleaned his apartment thoroughly and made sure everything was tidy. He then went to the library on campus to use the yahoo messenger so as to chat with his friends back home in Tayol and to send emails to siblings.

He made it a duty to update his family everyday via email about how he was getting on with life in Denmark. Mary, the eldest of the three sisters, was often the one responding to his emails.

Since his family had no internet broadband at home and due to the fact that mobile internet was not common at the time, the cheapest way for them to update him and vice versa was for one member of the family to collect information from everyone, go to the nearest internet café, and send all their messages via email and to print his emails and responses before taking them home and reading them to everyone.

While chatting with friends on the live chat messenger and sending emails to family members, he became anxious and nervous. He had sent a text to Gladys, informing her that he was in the library and asked her to meet him there when she finished her appointment.

Chapter 5: The Relationship with Gladys and Life as a Student

After having finished her appointment, Gladys made it to the library where she met Clement. She was magnificently dressed to impress him. She began by apologising to have made him wait longer. He indicated that he had been very fine as he had spent the time chatting with all of his sisters on yahoo messenger.

He had informed them that he would not be chatting a lot more often as he would be very busy from the next week when classes officially started whilst adding that he would try and send and respond to emails as often as possible.

When Gladys asked why he had done that, he responded that he would be much occupied with studies from the onset. As a result, he would need to be in the library studying during most of his spare time.

He added that even though his job was only eighteen hours per week, if he added the time to get to work, being at work and back to his apartment, it would add up to about twenty-five or thirty hours per week. So, he had to make good use of every spare time he had in studying.

With a massive smile on his face said, "I want to be able to spend more time with you". She blushed on hearing this and said " I am flattered".

She told him she was very impressed with his honesty and time consciousness and that the next time they had a rendezvous or date, she would make sure she was prompt. Upon hearing this, he started blushing too.

He could not believe what he had just heard her say, so he asked to confirm. "Did you just mention the word date?" he asked. Without any hesitation, she said "yes". From that moment, they felt very relaxed with each other as they walked to the Bilka supermarket.

After shopping, Clement decided that he would take a taxi as he had bought a lot of food and other household items; he did not want to inconvenience Gladys by having her carrying his goods.

To him, that would not create a very good impression of himself to her. She said she was happy to carry some of the goods and walk the twenty-five minutes journey to his apartment, but he politely turned down the offer.

He was determined to be a chivalrous gentleman who knew how to take good care of a lady. They finally got the taxi and went to his flat; it was just a 10 minutes drive by taxi and did not cost much.

Upon arriving at his apartment, the first thing she noticed was that, there had been changes in the positioning of all furniture in the flat.

He had bought a television, DVD recorder and a few DVD movies; a couple of the DVD movies were Nollywood and Bollywood movies and some of them were of famous African and Asian musicians which he said he had brought with him from Tayol.

She was also impressed by the fact that the apartment was much tidier than when she had first visited him. He smiled and said he had learned from her.

After they unpacked everything from the shopping bags, she said she wanted to get straight into cooking as she was hungry. He then played a DVD music video of one of Africa's famous musician: Brenda Fassie, titled "Vulindlela". She said she loved it and that it had been a while since she listened to African or Asian hits.

He soon joined her in the kitchen to help and to learn. She cooked fufu and palm nut soup with chicken. In addition to being very easy, it was very quick to cook as all the ingredients needed for cooking were already pre-made.

He just needed to learn about which ingredients were needed and the exact quantities needed for preparing the meal. While they were eating, he felt it was the right moment he should express his feelings towards her.

As he discovered, it was indeed a nerve-racking moment for him. So, he asked her to give him a few minutes and went into his bedroom.

He went there to revise on the notes he had written down from his research on the internet on," How to tell a girl that you love her".

Since, he felt that she was sending implicit signals of reciprocity; he was confident. He came back to the table and decided to be direct with her.

As he smiled at her, she asked while he was smiling. He told her that, it was because he was having the best moment of his life; he said he was glad she was there with him, before going on to add that he loved her and had always been attracted to her since the days at High School.

He even said that he had chosen to travel and study in Denmark because he wanted to be close to her. He asked if she could move in with him.

Getting Intimate

She listened very attentively. As he was talking, she got up from her chair as they had been facing each other; she walked towards him and gave him a kiss. He got up and they hugged each other with their lips locked to each other. She began to roll her tongue around his and he followed suit.

They were soon rolling their tongues around each other while their lips were locked firmly into each other. He began to tremble while they kissed, but she would not stop. This was the first time he had ever kissed anyone. The trembling stopped all of a sudden.

While they continued to kiss, he lifted her dress and took it off and she pulled off his shirt. They threw their clothes on the chair besides them. With their lips still locked firmly, he tried to use his fingers to unfasten her bra from behind, but had some difficulties doing so. He had never unclasped a bra before.

The kissing then stopped as she helped him unclasp her bra. Once she was done with that, they locked lips again, this time with even greater intensity. His hands were all over her breasts.

Enlarged dark nipples dotted both her breasts. There were so warm and responsive to his soft touch. As soon as his hands were upon her breasts; her kisses became deeper and more sensual.

His hands eventually moved from her breasts to her underwear. He slipped off his large fingers into her underwear as she slipped her entire right hand into his boxers and ended up massaging his large veiny penis. For about six minutes, they moaned in unison and continued with this routine. You could hear the sound of ah, ah, ah, ah, ah.

After ten minutes into this, she gave a loud scream, took a deep breath and began to smile. He was left wondering what had happened. She then went on her knees and gave him a blow job, and then a hand job until he came on her breasts.

They smiled and kissed each other gently. He went to the toilet and brought a white towel which they used to wipe and clean each other. They dressed up and went back to continue their meal.

Fully relaxed, he told her that, when she had gotten up from her chair, he had his heart beating very fast. He had felt she was going to walk away from his apartment. So, when she suddenly walked towards him, he was expecting to be slapped on the face and that it was an amazing feeling when she kissed him.

That evening, Clement and Gladys decided to invite Alex, Devine and Thomas. They wanted them to have dinner with them to share the delicious meal she had cooked, watch a movie and inform them that they were now seeing each other.

On the topic of her moving in with him, she said it was going to be a collective decision that she would have to make with her other friends.

When she said that, Clement did not think Alex, Devine and Thomas would be happy with her decision to move out.

With the thought that she might want to have a collective decision due to financial worries, as she relied on all four of them, including him, for financial assistance, he decided to guarantee that he would share fifty percent of his income with her.

Given that he had paid a year's rent as a one off and had everything in place for the entire, he pacified her and remarked that she no reason to be alarmed. He added that everything was in place to meet their financial obligations both in Denmark as well as to their respective families back in Tayol.

He also disclosed that he had enough money to sustain them for a whole year even if he wasn't working. At that moment, she hugged him again and they kissed without her uttering a word. Kissing was her way of indicating to him that she agreed. It was the first time Clement had fallen in love.

The sexual experience he had with Gladys somehow seemed to cloud his mind and judgement. He was making very quick decisions without thinking them through. The one thing he was certain about was that he had made up his mind to do everything possible to be with Gladys.

Joy Galore

Later that evening, Alex, Devine and Thomas visited them. They were very impressed with the changes he had made in his apartment. With the television and DVD recorder on with music playing, they were even more excited.

They thought that they now had a place where they could come around and enjoy some good Tayolese music and food. Gladys was lying very comfortably on the couch when they arrived.

They did not find it strange and that got him very surprised, but he chose to keep quiet.

He was unaware that Gladys had already informed Alex, Devine and Thomas about her attraction towards him and that when she had texted them to come over for meal that evening, she had also informed them about what had happened earlier during the day.

Gladys prepared and served the food for all of them and sat by Clement on the table as they began to eat. While they were eating, Clement decided it was finally time to inform them about the decision he had taken with Gladys.

As soon as he started talking, Thomas quickly interrupted and said they were all fine with everything, as long as Gladys was happy. They also expressed their desire to continue to share their income with Gladys until she got a job of her own.

This engulfed him with a feeling of joy. He proposed to give one key to Gladys and share the other between Alex, Thomas and Devine. He told them, they were welcomed at his apartment at any time even if he or Gladys were not there, as long as they informed him or Gladys in advance and as long as it wasn't after ten in the evening.

Laughing collectively, they said they understood him well and extended the same hospitality to him. He felt very happy at that moment.

As he and Gladys had nothing planned to do at the university the next day, he offered her to stay with him when the others were leaving.

She happily agreed. The next day, they went to Gladys' apartment to collect all her personal belongings. She then called Turbo and informed him she was moving out of his apartment and that Alex and the others would still be there.

Turbo was very happy for her and said that she was welcome to let him know whenever she was in a problem or even otherwise and that he would always be there for her.

She was ecstatic to hear those words from Turbo, knowing that she was not only guaranteed financial help in times of need, but was also loved and cared for by all of them. Most importantly, she had the love of Clement whom she had grown to love so much within a very short span of time.

Life as a student went on rather smoothly with Clement. Classes were five times per week, on week days and an average of four hours per day. He studied mostly in the library alongside Gladys.

They rarely stayed away from each other. Being a very dedicated student, he had no problems with studies. He always made top grades and was well admired by his lecturers.

His part time work went on brilliantly too, which meant that he was doing fantastic both academically and financially. He continued to send money every month to his family.

After three months of living in Denmark, he received an offer from a student loan credit card company of 30,000 DKK (approximately $5000).

He accepted the offer and obtained the credit card. He decided to keep it as a backup should he run into any financial difficulties. Living with Gladys felt very fulfilling; it felt to him like he had won a lottery of $1million. Both of them subscribed to a local gym and paid for a personal trainer.

This got Gladys into great shape and elevated her confidence too. Both of them joined the university health club as well. However, this decision was not premised on their keenness to seek advice on their health and wellbeing; it was strictly due to the fact that they were entitled to five free condoms each per week.

Since they frequently ran out of condoms, they convinced Alex to register at the health club too. This was because, they wanted him to collect his own share of the free condoms and hand it over to them.

After a spending six months with each other, they stopped frequenting the health club. They were now making love regularly without the use of condoms. However, then came a moment when Clement felt his whole world had come to a crashing end.

This was when Gladys felt sick and began to feel nauseous and eventually, vomit. He was petrified with the thought that she was pregnant. After consulting the doctor though, it was confirmed to be a mild sickness that is, gut infection (gastroenteritis), which only lasted for two days.

He continued to do well with studies and work. He also made sure to keep in touch with his entire family back home in Tayol, though not as frequently as he did when he initially arrived in Denmark.

While he continued to send them money every month, he reduced the amount. His dad's health condition improved as Clement sponsored his treatment at a private clinic.

He moved his sisters from private day school to the boarding school where he went to high school. He also provided money to his dad and uncle; they bought an even bigger land just close to the one they had sold. In addition, he sent some money to his elder brother Eric; he used it to open an electronics shop and enabled him to look after himself.

Since his business was doing well, he earned enough and moved out of the family home. Eric kept daily contact with his parents and sisters. He bought himself a phone and also kept weekly contact with Clement. Life seemed to progress just as Clement had envisioned for himself and his family.

Glady's Pregnancy and Clement's Worst Fears

Suddenly, Clement's worst fears came true; Gladys had indeed become pregnant. As soon as the pregnancy was confirmed, Clement became very stressed up. He felt his world was falling apart.

Meanwhile Gladys was happy to have conceived the baby as she was in her final year of studies. She knew that by the time she gave birth, she would have graduated.

Clement on the other hand, had other ideas. Plagued with the thought that this would be devastating news for family and that this might affect the progress of his studies, he asked Gladys to abort the child. Gladys was devastated to hear this.

She could not understand why he had rushed to that conclusion without thinking it through for a few days or weeks. Clement knew that a child could only be aborted before twelve weeks from conception as per Danish law.

With that knowledge, he had little time to waste. Given the fact that she knew he loved her, she understood the rationale behind his insistence. The reasons for Clement were very simple. He did not want to have a child out of wedlock; he wanted to focus on his career and was not prepared to be a father yet.

In Tayol, the first thought that subconsciously occurred to a lot of people when they saw a pregnant lady was, who was responsible, and what their plans were. Both Clement and Gladys were very much aware of this.

He knew that people would instantly have this thought about Gladys whether they meant it or not, or even if they meant no harm. To them, this predicament assumed great importance. He also knew there would be a lot of questions from friends and family members from Tayol, who would want to know if he would accept the pregnancy and/or would marry her.

He did not want people to think or ask these questions of whether it was a mistake, or if Gladys planned on keeping the pregnancy. And so on and so forth.

He was also thinking about his career. He had planned on completing his course in Denmark, move to the UK and complete the necessary training and studies to become a medical doctor.

He felt his job prospects and employability would be much more enhanced if he trained as a medical doctor in the UK. In addition, he was not ready to become a father yet.

Even though Denmark had been voted the happiest country in the world in the last few decades, Clement had deciphered that it was very tough to navigate the Danish system as a foreigner.

Clements's view was that adding another member to his existing family would make life tougher for him financially as he still had the commitment to send money back home in Tayol. Moreover, Gladys was not working. Clement was saving money as well that would be used to sponsor his studies should he eventually move to the UK.

Gladys on the other hand, had different plans. She had developed love for Denmark, given the fact that she had lived there longer than Clement and wanted to make it her home. She hoped to get a job once she graduated.

Since she was an unmarried partner to Clement who had a status of a foreign student on his visa, she thought she would be able to extend her initial six months visa given to graduates of non-EU/EEA/Swiss citizens upon the completion of their studies.

This would give her reasonable time to actively seek work. She was eligible to do so under the Danish immigration law. Since Denmark was notorious in offering very flexible working conditions to couples with children; placement was almost guaranteed in day care centres or day nurseries, if one had a job.

Gladys felt it was the best place to start a family life. She studied Masters in Economics and Business Administration- Sports and Event Management.

The company where she did her internship in Copenhagen were very impressed with her work upon completion and happily offered her a two year contract with the option of extension after her graduation if she intended to work with them.

She was to work as an events coordinator. Even though she only spoke, read, wrote and understood very little of the Danish language, it was not a prerequisite for the job offer.

Given that all these facts known to Clement, Gladys was quite perplexed. She could not understand why he would not change his mind. It seemed he had made up his mind on all aspects in his life and had no room for flexibility. She loved him very much and thought he did likewise.

The last thing she wanted to do was to entertain doubts about their bond. Questioning this would seem contrary to the spirit and essence their commitment. She started to worry a lot but did so privately, in the midst of a sleepless night, while jogging or showering. It felt like a serious betrayal.

For all that they had gone through together and the help he had offered her, she did not want to question whether Clement's values were aligned with hers enough to move forward, long past the salacious stage and into a lasting romantic attachment, or whether they wanted the same things out of life in practical, realistic terms, or whether she could imagine them parenting together and growing old alongside each other.

She did not want to impose all these questions because it seemed disrespectful to Clement and the life they had built together up to that moment.

After going through these myriad emotions and seeking advice from her parents back home as well as from a few other friends both in Denmark and across Europe, she decided not to abort the child. This was horrifying news for Clement.

The relationship was now at the verge of collapse; all their happiness had been turned upside down due to her pregnancy. The onus was now on Clement to come up with a secondary option. He needed sound advice and he needed it fast. He needed to be calm in order to deal with the increasingly urgent and difficult situation.

Chapter 6: Relationship Crisis

Gladys' decision not to abort the child had a huge impact on Clement. He was very depressed a week after the confirmation of her pregnancy. He had almost no communication with Gladys. He avoided being at home and spent most of his time in the library.

He was so depressed that he had to call in sick for work for two weeks. He lied to his doctor that he had abdominal pain and was given a sick note of two weeks. The sick note allowed him to get full payment of his work so that it did not affect him financially.

The greatest setback from this situation came from his examination results. He had some assignments during that period which were not dealt at a level that was expected out of him.

Much to his dismay, he ended up with a grade C in that module. Everyone who knew him personally, his lecturers, course colleagues, Alex, Divine, and Thomas noticed a drastic change in his character. He turned from being a very jovial person to being unusually reserved.

When asked if there was any problem, he lied to them about his made up sickness of abdominal pain. Since Gladys had not shared anything with his roommates, they did not know what was going on. Amidst the tumultuousness experienced by Clement, Gladys remained surprisingly calm. She carried out all her duties at home and her studies as if nothing had happened.

Even when Clement avoided sleeping on the bed and would sleep on the couch, she remained calm. She tried her best to avoid any arguments or confrontations. In a secret that remained unknown to Clement, this was not the first time Gladys had been pregnant. The first time she got pregnant was in Tayol.

This was at high school. She told no one about it. She used her school maintenance allowance and aborted the child at a local clinic. It was a horrifying experience for her, given her tender age.

She did not want to go through the same experience again since she considered herself to be mature enough to take care of the baby even without Clements' support.

She knew Turbo and her former roommates would be very willing to help her whenever she needed help. Plus, she was about to graduate and had a job in waiting.

Even though she loved Clement, the fact that there was now a baby in waiting had completely switched most of her love for him to the unborn baby. She was very determined about her decision not to abort the baby.

Getting Things Back on Track in Amsterdam

After ten weeks of the pregnancy, Clement figured out that she would not be aborting the child beyond twelve weeks due to Danish Law. He decided to book a weekend getaway with Gladys to Amsterdam.

His choice of Amsterdam was attributed to the act that of his course colleagues, Daan, a Dutch citizen, had planned to travel to Amsterdam for the weekend to visit his family.

Clement overheard Daan discussing his plan of the weekend gateway in the class with one of Daan's friends, so he approached Daan and asked if he could join him for the journey; Daan accepted the request.

They decided to rent a car as Daan could drive and because it was much more cost effective. The duration of the journey from SDU to Amsterdam was eight hours.

Clement and Gladys could travel to Amsterdam without needing a visa in wake of the Schengen agreement. Daan had also promised that he would spend at least three hours together while they were in Amsterdam to show them around the city. The hotels around the city centre were very cheap, so Daan helped him reserve one at a very affordable price.

The weekend getaway was primary to take the stress off Clement and to de-escalate the crisis he was having with Gladys. His last examination result had been very devastating for him.

He felt, if they could move away from the SDU area, go somewhere where they could have fun and be away from work and studies, they might be able to rejuvenate their love, reflect better on their differences and reach a consensus on the resolution to their crisis.

He was determined not to hurt Gladys' feelings; however, he also did not want to jeopardise his career prospects. The news they were to travel to Amsterdam was met with great excitement by Gladys.

She had never travelled out of Denmark since her arrival. The only place she had been to was Copenhagen, when she was doing her internship. The announcement of this short getaway injected some mojo back into their relationship.

For a short while, they seemed to forget about any crisis whatsoever. Clement was back sleeping on the bed. Her sex appeal was once again elevated. They even made love in the kitchen while she was cooking; this had never happened before.

It almost felt like they did not need the getaway weekend in the first place. He was still determined to go to Amsterdam. Not going, he thought, would be very detrimental to the newly rejuvenated mojo. Furthermore, he had deadline of just over a week left to know whether he would become a father or not.

The journey to Amsterdam made them pass Hamburg-Germany, which was half way of the entire journey. There, they had rest for two hours so that Daan could have a nap. While Daan was having a nap in the car by a free car park they had located very close to the Hamburg Zoo, Clement and Gladys decided to visit the Zoo for an hour.

It was just a 10 minute walk from the car park. The Hamburg Zoo, opened in 1863, has an elephant pavilion as well as tropical aquarium. Animals were seen in naturalistic enclosures and had massive spaces. Both of them were very excited to find elephants, sharks, monkeys, lions, tigers and a number of reptiles.

Even though most of these animals there were tropical animals coming from Africa and Asia, Clement and Gladys had never been so close to them animals, either in their natural environment or in a Zoo. This marked their first visit to the Zoo. They took many pictures of which they would later share with friends and family members. It was the beginning of a fantastic weekend.

From Hamburg, it took another four hours drive to reach Amsterdam. They were all very knackered upon arriving in Amsterdam. Daan was the most tired as he had done all the driving.

He dropped them off at their hotel which was very close to the city centre and only around 15 minutes drive from his family's home. As it was about seven in the evening, he drove home to see his parents and siblings.

He promised to come back around eleven in the morning, so that he could take them out and show them around Amsterdam.

Rediscovering Erotic Passion

They checked in at the hotel, had a shower together and decided to take a walk into the city centre which was situated at a five-minute walking distance.

At the city centre, they had a meal and a bottle of wine in a restaurant.

Clement wanted to try a Dutch snack, so he ordered Kibbeling; a snack consisting of battered chunks of fish, commonly served with a mayonnaise-based garlic sauce, lemon or tartar sauce; usually cod.

They were every bit as delicious as they looked. From there, he decided to walk up to De Wallen, an area which houses the world famous RED LIGHT DISTRICT. It was hard to miss the crowded district; he did not have to ask for directions, with all the windows blazing in fluorescent red lights.

In De Wallen, prostitution, the oldest profession in the world, is legal with the exception of street prostitution. They were informed by a local tour guide that female sex workers of all nationalities could be found here, often sitting in window parlours vying for the attention of the passing men.

The embarrassing thought of finding a Tayolese sex worker did cross Clement's mind. He could not believe that men will actually pay to have sex with strangers, but he understood why some women chose such jobs. The place was filled with groups of rowdy men dressed in similar football t-shirts who spoke very good English.

When he asked them where they were from, he was told they came from England into Amsterdam to watch their team, Manchester United play against AFC Ajax in the Champions League.

There were other groups of rowdy men out in the town for a bachelor party, giggling girls on a hen night as well as couples and families going about their everyday business.

They were also informed through a tourist information notice posted on a board right in front of the tourist office at the city centre (which was close at the time) that, Amsterdam was the free land where prostitution and marijuana were legal, but it was definitely not the land of lawlessness, as it is dotted with coffee shops and boasts of not just one but three Red Light District areas. However, the streets were patrolled by the police at all times.

This meant that both the Red light area and the city in general were safe both during the day and night, apart from the ubiquitous pickpockets that roam around. Surprisingly, Gladys did not get upset being in the area. She had heard of the RED LIGHT DISTRICT before and all the naughtiness surrounding it, so it was more a case of being inquisitive and experiencing the place firsthand as a tourist with Clement than anything else.

She did not feel threatened or harmed. It was all part of the weekend getaway experience.

After spending about one hour walking around the area, Gladys became exhausted. She needed to go to bed, so they walked back to the hotel. When they got back into their room, she said "Thank you for the amazing experience of the day" to Clement.

Having been around the RED LIGHT DISTRICT and seeing all those semi-naked girls, Clement had developed a very high libido. Even though he knew Gladys was very tired, he couldn't sleep and wait for the next day without making love to her.

After undressing completely, they went to bed naked and lay in the spoons position. This position made them fit together perfectly on the small size double bed.

This cuddling position was intended to maximise their intimacy and comfort. It allowed them to snuggle into each other like spoons inside the drawer. At that precise moment, both of them wanted to make passionate love to each other.

Pulling her hair from behind with his powerful left arm, he gripped her butt firmly with his right hand. He then inserted his six inches long prick into her from behind and slowly began to move back and forth like a pendulum. Both felt like as if they were in a fairyland.

He then stopped after about five minutes and climbed down the bed. She did not say anything and just observed his next move in anticipation. She knew that, Clement was an intelligent man and would have thought of a better idea on enjoying the sex even better.

He removed his phone charger with the phone that was plugged to the mains electricity supply slightly far away from the bed and plugged it to the mains electricity supply that was close to the bed.

This was because he wanted to have constant access to the phone so as to use it and play audio sounds that he had downloaded. He opened the file manager of the phone, went to the audio music section and selected Celine Dion-The Power of Love.

He played and left it on repeat. After doing so, he adjusted himself in the same spoons position; Gladys turned immediately and they faced the same direction. This time, he held her very tight. It felt like they had used superglue to bond themselves together.

With the music on very high volume, he again inserted his almost a little bit more than six inches "bazooka" into her from behind. While following the rhythm of the track, he slowly stroked back and forth.

Soon, he began to increase the speed of his movements, contradicting the rhythm of the track. You could hear the squeal and low moaning sounds of "...ah, ah, ah, ah, ah, ah, ah"; Gladys would intermittently groan "yes, deeper, deeper, harder, deeper, harder, harder, Oh baby, fuck, yes, yes, yes".

This lasted for about thirty minutes and then, there was massive groaning as he shot his load inside her. He became very weak after this and had to get some water to drink. The entire room was stinking of pussy fart and Clement's body odour, as he was sweating profusely. Gladys did not cum during their intercourse, although she pretended she did because she was very knackered and wanted to sleep.

Moreover, she did not want Clement to feel that he had not done a proper job. Clement went to the bathroom, took a towel and wiped his entire body and used another one to wipe Gladys' body.

When done, he climbed back to the bed, kissed Gladys and touched her boobs; it got his "bazooka" firmly hard yet again. He inserted it inside her as they reverted to their previous position. He gripped her boobs from behind with both hands, said "good night, I love you", Gladys said the same and, they slept off.

They woke up early, had a quickie and a warm soapy bath; they had to hurryingly dress and rush to the hotel breakfast hall for their breakfast buffet at nine, given that it was an all inclusive breakfast lodge. If they failed to make it for breakfast on time, it would lead to a reduction in their planned budget for Amsterdam as the cost of eating out was just too much for them.

After breakfast, Clement felt it was the right time for them to discuss and resolve their differences. They finished eating breakfast just before ten am and had over an hour left for Daan to come and take them around the city. At the hotel room, they both went back and lay on the bed facing each other.

An Honest Conversation

As it turned out, this was the moment Clement had been waiting for. Even before he could say anything, Gladys said: "I have to keep the baby." She informed him of what had happened to her before when she was at high school in Tayol, and how aborting her first conceived child had affected her mentally.

She also reiterated the fact that, life in Denmark was amazingly better than Tayol; it had a government which catered for its people, the standard of living was high and things were very comfortable in general.

She said she wanted to make Denmark her new home, and raise a family there. She was very hopeful of getting the job she had been promised after graduation and had plans of becoming a Danish Citizen in the future.

To this, Clement had no response; it seemed as if the getaway trip he had planned to convince Gladys to abort had instead got him convinced about not aborting the child. He had to respect her wishes.

He said the last few days had really made him appreciative of the love they had for each other and that he would work hard to be a great father to the child. The only impediment was that he was determined to complete his medical doctorate programme in the UK.

He said, he would go there, complete the training and move back to Denmark, ensuring that he would frequently travel to Denmark to visit her and the child.

To this, she said she was happy with his plans. If offered the job, she remarked that she would be able to look after the baby on her own, as Denmark had an efficient child day care system that would assist her with the child.

Another supportive point was that the majority of employers offered flexible working hours to people with children. She was confident that her new employers would offer her a flexible shift.

With all their differences taken care of, it was now left for Clement to inform his family and friends about the situation. He had to inform them about Gladys, the fact that she was pregnant and that he was ready to become a father.

They still had about fifteen minutes left to wait for Daan, so they decided to have another quickie. When he arrived at exactly eleven in the morning to take them to the city, they were ready and waiting for him. He announced to them that, his parents had asked him to bring them over for lunch. Daan's mother was particularly keen to meet his new friends.

She was very excited as Daan was very reserved; he did not have many friends growing up. They were even happier that he had integrated and made friends with people of different nationalities. Clement and Gladys readily accepted the invitation for lunch. They knew it would save them the money they had to spend for lunch.

An Exciting Day Beckons

Daan began by saying that, the best way they could have navigated through Amsterdam was by renting bikes to tour the city at a comfortable pace. Renting a bike for a day would cost about $18.

They could bike along the historic canals, visit favourite museums, such as the Rijksmuseum and Anne Frank House, and perhaps spend some time riding in the picturesque Dutch countryside.

This wasn't feasible because Gladys could not ride a bike. So, they decided to buy the " I Amsterdam city card". This cost $70 each. Clement opted to pay for these, including one for Daan as he had gone out of his way to help them with almost all aspects of their journey and stay in Amsterdam.

Being a gentleman, Daan thanked Clement and said he appreciated the amazing gesture, but that he would love to pay for his own card as it cost a lot. Clement and Gladys then vocalised their appreciation of his gesture of taking the time he should have been spending with his family to serve as their tour guide.

They were all shocked that the " I Amsterdam card" made them eligible for free admission to 44 museums and attractions in Amsterdam. They could also ride the city transport system (trams, buses and metro) for free for the entire duration of up to 24hrs. When they read further from the "I am Amsterdam card" brochure, they were even more elated.

Daan had never used the card before as him; his friends and his family often used their bikes to tour the city. Inevitably, he too was shocked.

They found that they could get free and discounted admission to sights outside Amsterdam city centre, go on a free canal cruise and see Amsterdam as it's meant to be seen, take advantage of 25% discount offers at a host of restaurants and cafés, explore Amsterdam by bike, boat or scooter at discounted rates, discover Dutch icons, such as beer, diamonds, cheese, and windmill and use the card for sites in Haarlem, Zaanse, Schans, Volendam and much more.

With all these listings, Clement became visibly excited. He was particularly keen on boarding the canal cruise and enjoying the Heineken experience, which was one of Amsterdam's most authentic and famous attractions.

Located in the centre, the old factory used to manufacture all of the brand's beer until 1988 when the main production line was moved to a larger facility outside the city due to the product's overwhelming demand.

It currently operates as a museum and a tourist attraction that has been visited by millions of people from all over the world ever since it opened its doors in 2001. This included an interactive self-guided walk through the factory which they undertook, a Heineken tasting session which Clement and Daan gladly experienced, fun information about the company's history and the Heineken logo and much more.

Gladys meanwhile was keener to visit the museums, especially the Van Gogh and the Rijksmuseum, which offered a representative overview of the Dutch art and history from the Middle Ages onwards as well as of the major aspects of European and Asian art.

On the other hand, the Van Gogh museum is to the works of Vincent van Gogh and his contemporaries. Clement was very surprised by this revelation; he did not know that Gladys was a big fan of the works of arts.

They started the tour by boarding the canal cruise before visiting the museums, gardens; their final stop was to live the Heineken experience.

They were able to see the gigantic copper tanks that were used to brew the original Heineken beer. At the end of the Heineken Brewery Tour which lasted around one hour, they were able to enjoy two complimentary drinks while relaxing in the bar.

Meeting Daan's Parents

Non-alcoholic drinks were also available, so Gladys decided to go for those drinks. People could try their hands at drafting their own Heineken, so Clement and Daan tried making theirs which actually tasted great, but nothing like Heineken. It was a fantastic experience to say the last. From there, they boarded a bus to Daan's house for lunch.

At Daan's home, his mother and father welcomed them with a lot of enthusiasm. They made Clement and Gladys feel very comfortable and showed them around the entire house.

Daan' mother cooked a simple and straightforward traditional Dutch cuisine; meat and potatoes, supplemented with seasonal vegetables. She had also used a lot of bread with toppings of cheese.

When food was served on the table, there were two bottles of expensive French wine Châteauneuf-du-Pape and tea. After the meal, Clement and Gladys thanked the family for their kind hospitality.

In particular, they heaped praise on Daan's mother for the food, they enjoyed so much. Daan's father did not drink the wine; he drank tea instead because he had volunteered as the designated driver for the night and promised to take Clement and Gladys back to their hotel.

After dinner, while they were having wine, Daan's mother proposed that they spend the night at their house as they had two guest rooms, but Clement objected to it.

He pointed out that he had already paid for the entire stay and that it was too late to cancel their reservation and get a refund. However, this was not the main reason why he did not want to spend the night at Daan's house.

'The Night' of Making Passionate Love

In reality, he wanted to have another splendid love making night with Gladys at the hotel. Since Gladys had the tendency of moaning and screaming during sex, he thought that having sex at Daan's house would be disrespectful to Daan and his family.

Moreover, he was not prepared to wait another day, since they were travelling back to Denmark the following day.

After Daan's father dropped them at the hotel, they thanked him and promised him they would visit them again in the future with Daan and that they will be more than happy to spend their stay with his family.

Upon reaching their room, without wasting a minute, Gladys slowly and seductively removed her jacket and threw it on the couch, as she climbed onto the bed; she then unbuttoned her pink shirt to show her uncovered left breast as she had no bra.

She started to rub her feet together and then rolled around on the bed. Clement stood there watching her in much excitement and anticipation. Walking towards her, he climbed on the bed and started kissing her before sucking her breasts.

He then told her it might be inappropriate to continue to have sex as she was pregnant, since it could be bad for the unborn baby. She smiled and said there was no such scientific research to substantiate his statement. She was trying to compensate for the previous night.

He carried her off the bed and was standing with her legs long over his arms and him holding her against his chest. At that moment he was topless with a big fake tattoo running up his right arm which he had inked from a tattoo shop while touring around the city that day.

He slowly dismounted and let her down. She then went down on her knees and started to unbutton his pants.

His cock was huge, dark and veiny, which made her extremely excited. She started to caress and lick his cock. She said she had no idea that she could handle such a huge cock every day.

Her pussy was tiny compared to his massive dick which curved a bit like a banana. He then skilfully used his mouth to pull her pants down. She was mostly shaved with very short pubic hair.

Carrying her back to the bed, he pushed her legs up in the back over and beyond herself so that her ass was in the air; he slowly inserted his huge dark brown cock up and down her pussy, while moving back and forth to shove the entire length of his penis. He leaned over her and simultaneously kissed her very passionately.

She looked like she could come already. Going up and down, he was cautiously slow even as she kept moaning very loud and saying " yes yes yes, give it to me". She started rubbing her pussy and screaming even louder than ever before. After a few minutes, she started to quiver and then, there was orgasm.

He moved over and laid down on the bed with his back on the bed while she leaned forward to him and gave him a blowjob for a few minutes. He then turned her over for doggy style. While he was behind her, she began rubbing her pussy again with her hands.

After about a quarter of an hour, it seemed she was ready to come again. Her whole body was shaking and trembling in sexual ecstasy and she was extraordinary loud; one could think she was being physically abused. She kept saying " yes, yes, yes, omg, omg, omg".

While still f****** her from behind, he sat up a bit, put his hands around her down against the bed, with her head heading over the edge. He increased the speed almost as if he had made up his mind to destroy her pussy. He kept changing positions, from kneeling to legs out while speeding and slowing down, and f****** her in doggy style.

As he moved faster, it looked like he might come soon. He then moved his hands off her ass and groaned while f****** her even harder. She turned her head sideways towards him and said " you have completely destroyed me."

He started f****** her slowly, still from behind and kept saying " this is completely wrong", in reference to her pregnancy. He was going deeper and deeper with his black balls squeezing tightly against her pussy. She started saying "you're crazy, you're crazy, go on, go on, ah, ah ,ah, ah ,ah"

They then climbed down the bed and he laid down on the floor with his legs bent over the side of the lounge, as he supported her legs underneath. She was bouncing up and down on his cock and was about to come again.

He then looked up with a satisfied smile before laying down on his head and back again.

She was saying "yes, yes, yes, yes " all the while rubbing her pussy at a much faster and intense pace. She finally came while trembling and collapsing into his arms. He then pulled her legs back towards him so that she was sitting on his belly and started f****** her harder.

They changed position with him f****** her while standing up. Her arms were wrapped around his neck and her legs were hung-over his arms.

As he kissed her, he also moved forward and put her up against the wall, where they continue f****** . He backed away from the wall and then started bouncing her up and down his cock. He groaned pre-orgasmically and then started to put her down to the ground.

They kissed passionately as he dismounted her. She knelt down and took his "BIG GUY" straight into her mouth. She gave him a blowjob for a few moments, pulled out his "BIG GUY" and shot his load all over her face.

They smiled at each other, went to the bathroom and had a sensual shower together. Thereafter, they slept naked together in their favourite "spoons position."

The next day, they woke up early feeling extremely energised and totally into each other. They showered together with Gladys giving Clement a quick blowjob.

After breakfast, they checked out immediately as Daan was waiting for them at the hotel car park, so that they could commence their journey back to Denmark. On their way back to Denmark, after about three hours of driving (just before they reached Hambury), Clement asked Daan if he could stop at any field close by and give him a few driving lessons.

He was planning to drive for at least an hour during the course of the journey. Gladys wasn't comfortable with this idea as it was illegal. She was also scared about a potential accident. Unsurprisingly, Daan agreed to this request. After three and a half hours of driving, they arrived in Bremen, Germany.

After Daan located a field around, they got Gladys out of the car and dropped her at a coffee shop close by. He then spent an hour giving Clement a driving lesson. From there, they continued their journey.

Clement was given the opportunity to drive for an hour. He wasn't really bothered about being caught by the police because he had obtained a Tayol driver's license before travelling to Denmark by bribing an official at the ministry of transport.

It was common for people in Tayol to obtain a driver's license even without undergoing the theoretical part of the exams or passing the practical part of the test. All they had to do was to bribe an official.

Clement was under the impression that, in Denmark, his license was valid for a year before he was legally required to get a Danish one, which would be valid in all EU countries.

However, this was far from the truth since the Danish law only allows 90 days for a foreigner with a foreign license outside the EU to drive after taking up residence. The good news for him however, was that he was not caught by the police while driving from Bremen towards Denmark.

They arrived safely in Denmark. Both of them were very thankful to Daan as he dropped them at their home and went straight to the car rental agency to hand over the car.

They felt very satisfied with their trip, as they had resolved all their differences amicably and found solutions to all the issues concerning Clements' career prospects in the UK and Gladys' pregnancy. Moreover, they had reinvigorated their love and passion for each other.

Chapter 7: Clements' Performance at University and Planning for the UK

Clement wasn't a typical student. He was very focused and disciplined. He spent most of his time in the library while on campus and attended every single lecture. His assignments and study tasks were always submitted at least two days prior to the deadline.

Even though the Odense campus offered a varied student life with a wealth of opportunities for both social and study-related experiences, Clement was 95% more concerned with a study-oriented experience.

There were about 23,000 students and 3,100 employees studying and working at the Odense campus where Clement attended most of his lectures.

The campus covered approximately four square kilometres, making it nearly twice the size of the Principality of Monaco. Clement and Gladys often found it most convenient, as it was very spacious and quiet, without causing any distractions to study at the woodland on campus which covered close to twenty percent of the area.

Given that almost all the students studied under a single roof, Clement had to encounter many different students from a variety of different programmes and nationalities every day. However, he was primarily interested in interacting with those who were more into study-related projects than being part of a bigger social circle.

After the trip to Amsterdam, Daan became a very close friend of Clement; they were also studying the same programme. Clement motivated Daan to attend classes sincerely and complete all his assignments on time.

Time management was most important to Clement. In addition to his studies, he was also occupied with his part-time job; plus, he had to spend quality time with Gladys.

However, it was not particularly difficult for Clement as he was extremely disciplined. Studying and getting top grades remained his first priority. This reflected well on all his exams results as well.

Brilliance in Preparing for Assignments

With regard to the assignments, he was simply brilliant. He wrote them legibly, orderly and coherently. He supplied all the necessary commentary that made his work clearer and easier to understand.

For this reason, his lecturers loved reading his work. They were always amazed at the level of research he put into his work. He always went the extra mile when it concerned his study tasks.

One thing which he habitually did after getting his results and finding out if he had achieved top grades, was to always go over the solutions provided by the instructor if it was available, even if he did well.

The instructors sometimes demonstrated more efficient methods or provided useful information that he never thought of, which, in turn, helped him in other assignments.

For his exams preparations, he prioritised each coursework material based on its importance and concentrated his studies on the most important topics. He had learnt from practical experience that most instructors only had a limited amount of time to test the knowledge of their students.

Moreover, there were topics he knew that he would be tested on, and nine out of ten times he was right.

He often studied with Daan or alone in the library during the exams. Most often, his best time for studies was around 4am in the morning. Given the fact that he was working, he took most of his annual leave during the exam period. That allowed him to have more time to focus on his studies.

Clement always summarised or outlined the course/text material in his own words after reading every single topic. This not only allowed him to examine the subject matter in great detail; it also provided a compendium to review just prior to the exam.

He always played it safe by doing extra research on every topic even when he was asked not to do so by the instructor. Clement did this because he did not want be in a situation wherein he found himself not knowing the answer to any question.

He was excellent at going through old exams materials, especially if he had been informed by former students who were taught by the same instructor with the same set of questions. Owing to the efficacy of his preparation, he rarely faced exam-related anxieties. He always convinced himself that he had done all that he needed to do.

Even with that mentality, he was never complacent. Clement always felt excited before the start of every exam, as opposed to feeling anxious.

He was always confident in his ability to do well in every exam. He never disliked any modules or topic. If he found a topic tough to understand, he would research more on it and would meet the course instructor privately for further explanation.

He read and eventually mastered various books on how to succeed in assessments and examinations. This helped him a lot in preparing for and writing the exams.

During exams, he made sure he read the instructions thoroughly and carefully. He would skim over the entire exam prior to beginning his work; problems were not necessarily done in order.

Problems that he felt very confident about were dealt with at the start to get them out of the way.

Observations were always based on how the questions were weighed. He would also direct his efforts to where he believed he would pick up the maxim number of points. This did not necessarily mean that he attempted the most heavily weighed problems first; instead, it meant he solved the problems and answered questions that would accumulate points at the fastest rate.

In fact, he knew there was a great chance that these would not be the most heavily weighed questions in the first place, since many instructors did not like assigning significantly greater or lesser points to a single problem, thereby underweighting the harder problems and over weighing the easier ones.

Before starting to answer any questions, he took a few seconds to think them through. This is because a small investment in time at the beginning helped him save time in the longer run as it sometimes encouraged him to find a more efficient method of answering the question.

He did precisely what was requested. He did not waste any time doing things that he would not receive credit for. Unless explicitly required, he did not rewrite the exam questions on his answer sheet. He paced himself well through the exam. On a 100 minutes exam worth 100 points, he would accumulate 1 point per minute.

As a result, a 30 points problem would be completed in 30 minutes or less, especially on questions that were easier. He did this at the start of each exam. He wrote something meaningful at beginning of each question and would constantly check the time.

Towards the end of the exams, if he was short on time, especially as he would have been dealing with the tough questions towards the end, he would write something meaningful for every remaining question and then move on to the next one to accumulate as many points as possible.

In order to gain even more points, he would sometimes write bullet point answers and outline the steps he would have written if he had more time to continue. This enabled him to showcase his work better and made clearer reasoning for the instructors to offer him partial credit.

He always went over his work if he had the time to do so. Barring the exam he wrote when he was stressed up with Gladys' pregnancy and achieved a low grade, he achieved the highest grades in all of his other modules.

After completing his course, he had just three months to prepare and move to the UK. He applied and got an unconditional offer of admission at the University on Cardiff, Wales with full sponsorship of doing postgraduate research: BioMed Doctoral Training PhD project in the School of Medicine. He was elated after receiving the offer.

Gladys was very happy for him too. He and Gladys organised a massive party and invited all their friends in and around Denmark. His entire family back home in Tayol were also extremely happy.

He sent them some money for them to organise a massive party and celebrate.

Gladys had not yet given birth, but had started work with the events company where she had done her internship when Clement was offered the admission. Since his doctorate training was fully sponsored, he decided that he would leave a third of the money he had saved for self sponsorship of his doctorate training programme with Gladys.

He sent another third of the amount to his family and decided to use the remaining amount to take driving lessons and obtain a drivers license before travelling to the UK and to pay for his flight, accommodation and buy a car upon his arrival in the UK.

He promised Gladys that he would work even harder when he got to the UK and would frequent Denmark to visit her and the baby.

Gladys was due delivery a month after Clement' programme at the Cardiff University would have started, so he decided he would go to the UK and would make sure to be back with Gladys during her delivery. Sorting everything out, he finally left for the UK.

The next volume "Deception" that I am currently writing describes different facets of Clement's life in the UK and his challenges. Since he was fully sponsored for his study programme and could communicate very well in English, he makes many new friends.

Soon, he gets complacent and starts to drink a lot. Gladys finally gives birth to their baby even as Clement breaks all the promises he made to Gladys.

He starts living a playboy lifestyle, dating one girl after another. Expect many more twists and turns in his career prospects, his relationship with Gladys and his child and the myriad problems he gets embroiled into during his stay in the UK. Find out all that and more about Clement and his life in "Deception."

I will be grateful if after reading, you take a minute or two of your time to leave your review. This would allow me to spend less time marketing this novella, and more time writing the next volume. Your reviews would also educate me on the positives and negatives about my writing thereby enabling the next volume to be an even better thriller than this one.

Thank you very much for taking your time to read this novella.

Made in the USA
Lexington, KY
07 May 2018